Feelings

I'M Sad

and other tricky feelings

Clare Hibbert
Illustrated by Simona Dimitri

Evans

Published by Evans Brothers Limited
2A Portman Mansions, Chiltern Street, London W1U 6NR

© Evans Brothers Limited 2010
Concept devised for Evans Brothers by Clare Hibbert

Editor: Clare Hibbert
Designer: Sandra Perry
Picture researcher: Sophie Schrey
Illustrator: Simona Dimitri (Milan Illustration Agency)
Sign language artist: Rob Perry

British Library Cataloguing in Publication Data
Hibbert, Clare, 1970-
Sad. -- (Feelings)
1. Sadness—Juvenile literature.
I. Title II. Series
152.4-dc22

ISBN-13: 9780237541996

Printed & bound in China by New Era Printing Co. Ltd.

**The signing instructions in this book follow British Sign Language.
The visual instructions show a mirror image to make it easier for
you to practise your own signing in front of a mirror.**

CONTENTS

Sad ~~~~~~~~~~ 4

Jealous ~~~~~~~~ 6

Shocked ~~~~~~ 8

Upset ~~~~~~~~ 10

Scared ~~~~~~~ 12

Worried ~~~~~~ 14

Cross ~~~~~~~ 16

Mean ~~~~~~~ 18

Shy ~~~~~~~ 20

Notes for adults ~~~~ 22

Sign language index ~~~ 24

Index ~~~~~~~ 24

Sad

sniff
sob

4

| sad | jealous | shocked | upset |

Jealous

Granny let Archie water the plants. I felt **jealous**.

6

sad

jealous

shocked

upset

7

Shocked

yikes

In my dream, my dog turned into a wolf. I felt **shocked**!

8

sad   jealous   shocked   upset

slobber, slobber

scared

worried

cross

mean

shy

Upset

When my cousin moved away, I felt very **upset**. But now he can visit me.

sad   jealous   shocked   upset

10

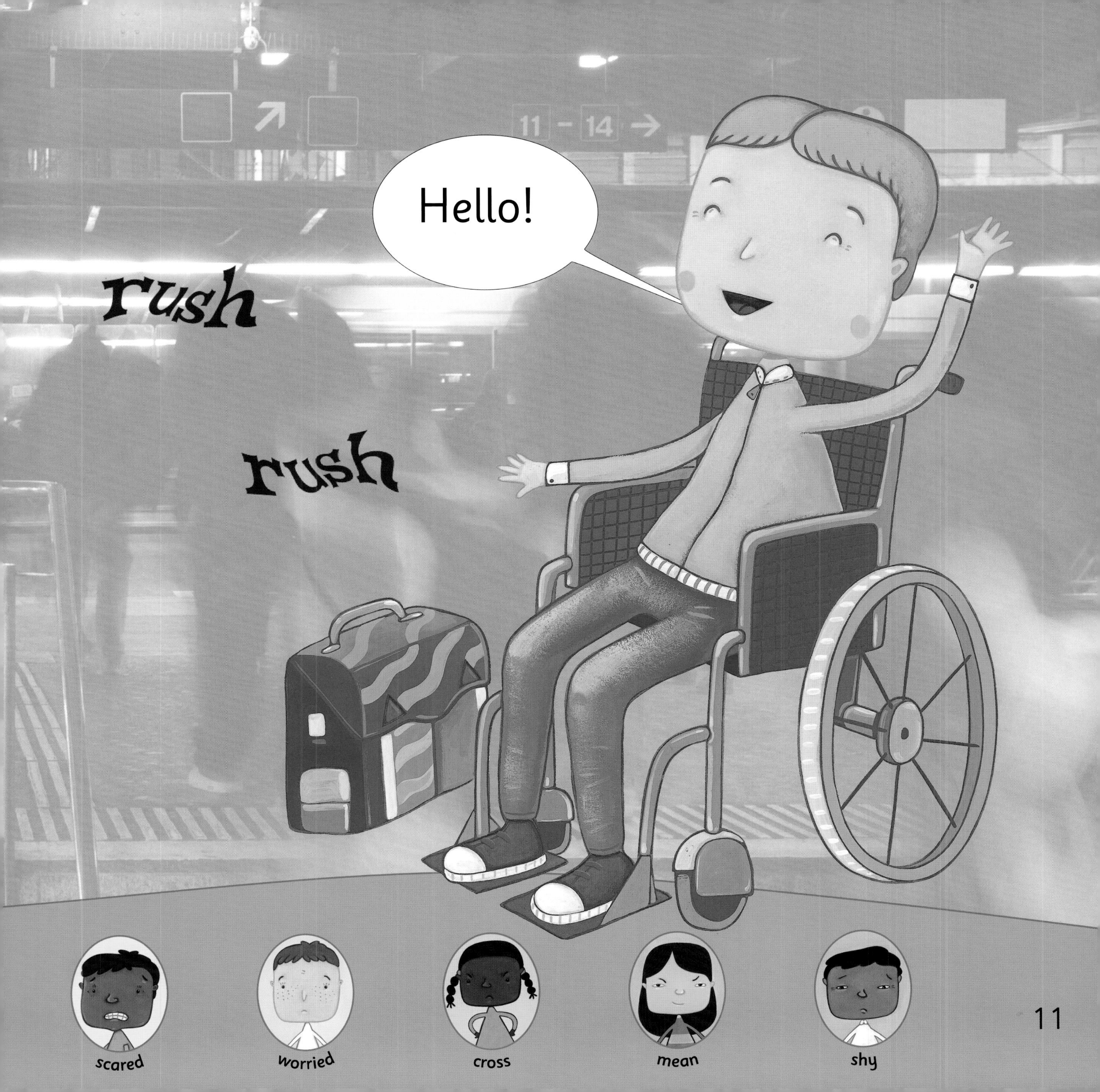
11 - 14
Hello!
rush
rush
scared
worried
cross
mean
shy

Scared

creak,
creak

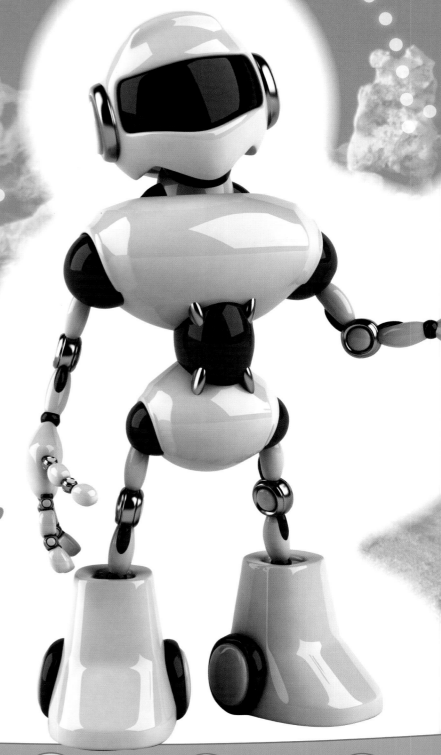

sad

jealous

shocked

upset

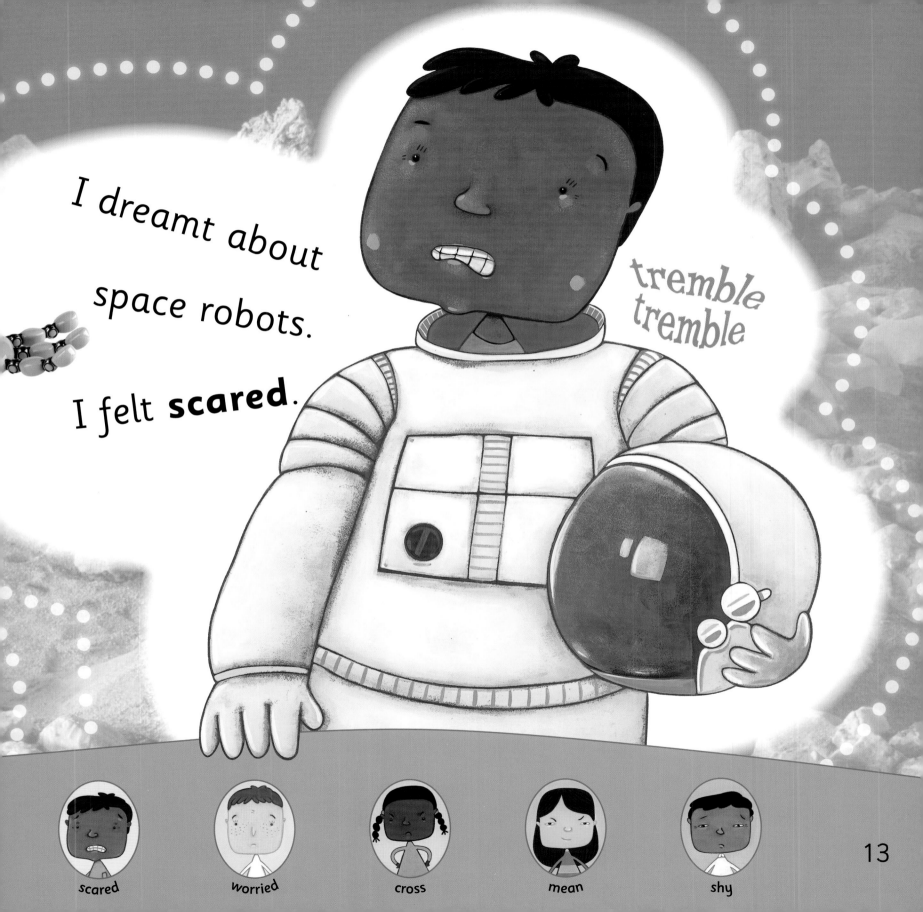

Worried

chatter chatter

sad

jealous

shocked

upset

15

Cross

I spilt water all over my picture. I felt **cross**.

sad

jealous

shocked

upset

scared

worried

cross

mean

shy

21

Notes for adults

The **Feelings...** series has been designed to support and extend the learning of young children. The books link in to the Early Years curriculum and beyond. Find out more about Early Years and reading with children from the National Literacy Trust (www.literacytrust.org.uk).

The **Feelings...** series helps to develop children's knowledge, understanding and skills in key social and emotional aspects of learning (SEAL), in particular empathy, self-awareness and social skills. It aims to help children understand, articulate and manage their feelings. Visit http://nationalstrategies.standards.dcsf.gov.uk/node/87009 to find out more about SEAL.

Titles in the series:
I'm Happy and other fun feelings looks at positive emotions
I'm Sad and other tricky feelings looks at uncomfortable emotions
I'm Tired and other body feelings looks at physical feelings
I'm Busy a feelings story explores other familiar feelings

The **Feelings...** books offer the following special features:

1) **matching game**
   a border of expressive faces gives readers the chance to hunt out the face that matches the emotion covered on the spread;
2) **signing instructions**
   each spread includes clear visual instructions for signing the emotion (these follow British Sign Language standard – visit britishsignlanguage.com for more information about this organisation);
3) **fantasy scenes**
   since children often explore emotion through stories, dreams and their imaginations, two emotions (in this book, 'shocked' and 'scared') are presented in a fantasy setting, giving the opportunity to examine intense feelings in the safety of an unreal context.

Making the most of reading time
When reading with younger children, take time to explore the pictures together. Ask children to find, identify, count or describe different objects. Point out colours and textures. Pause in your reading so that children can ask questions, repeat your words or even predict the next word. This sort of participation develops early reading skills.

Follow the words with your finger as you read. The main text is in Infant Sassoon, a clear, friendly font designed for children learning to read and write. The thought and speech bubbles and sound effects add fun and give the opportunity to distinguish between levels of communication.

Extend children's learning by using this book as a springboard for discussion and follow-on activities. Here are a few ideas:

Pages 4–5: I feel sad

Make a story sack themed around losing a favourite toy. You could include *Dogger* by Shirley Hughes, *Elmer and the Lost Teddy* by David McKee and *Where's My Teddy?* by Jez Alborough. Encourage children to set up a teddy bears' picnic – they could make pretend food out of modelling dough.

Pages 6–7: I feel jealous

Talk about situations in which the children have felt jealous. What made them feel better? Discuss some strategies for joining in, instead of feeling left out.

Pages 8–9: I feel shocked

If you have a group of children, why not play 'What's the time, Mr Wolf?'. One child is Mr Wolf and stands with their back turned. The others stand at the opposite end of the room, garden or playground. Each time the children call out 'What's the time, Mr Wolf?', the wolf calls out a time between one and 12 o'clock, and the children advance that many steps. But if the wolf calls out 'Dinner time!' the children must run back to the start – if the wolf catches one, that child is the new wolf.

Pages 10–11: I feel upset

Ask children to imagine a best friend moving away. How would they stay in touch? Give each child a sheet of paper so they can 'write' a letter to this faraway friend. Divide the paper into eight. In seven of the spaces, write the day of the week, and encourage the children to draw a picture or write a few words to describe what they did on that day. In the last space, they can copy the words "What did *you* do? Love [their name]".

Pages 12–13: I feel scared

Give each child some card and felt-tips and ask them to draw the scariest monster imaginable. Help them to cut their picture into six pieces to make a jigsaw. You can make longer-lasting scary-monster jigsaws with a laminating machine.

Pages 14–15: I feel worried

Provide wooden pegs, glue and colourful scraps of cloth for making worry dolls. Worry dolls are a tradition in Guatemala. At bedtime, children tell a worry to the doll and place it under their pillow. The idea is that the doll takes care of the worry as the child sleeps (sometimes, parents take away the doll).

Pages 16–17: I feel cross

How could the girl stop feeling cross? By making an even better picture! Encourage the children to collaborate on a mural, using paints or collage materials, that shows themselves having fun.

Pages 18–19: I feel mean

Teach some noisy songs that children can sing at home in the bath – far more fun than annoying an older sibling or being mean to a younger one. 'Five little ducks' is a good one!

Pages 20–21: I feel shy

Dressing up and role play are great ways of helping children overcome their shyness. While wearing a costume, they can leave their shy self behind and become someone else – for example, a superhero or an explorer. Animal masks are a useful prop for imaginative, confidence-building play, allowing the children to practise animal moves and make appropriate noises.

Sign language

cross **16**

jealous **6**

mean **18**

sad **4**

scared **12**

shocked **8**

shy **20**

upset **10**

worried **14**

Index

a
aquarium **14, 15**

b
bath time **18, 19**

g
gardening **6, 7**

p
painting **16, 17**

s
space robots **12, 13**
starting school **20, 21**

t
teddy **4, 5**
train station **10, 11**

w
wolves **8, 9**

Credits

The publisher would like to thank the following for permission to reproduce their images:
Dreamstime: cover and 4–5 (Moth), 18–19 (Cbsva); **iStockphoto:** 4 (ivanastar), 6–7 (skhoward), 6 (wwing), 8–9 (AVTG), 8 basket (DNY59), 8 bone (jclegg), 10–11 (assalve), 10 (Ziva_K), 12–13 (Christian Lohman), 12bl (julos), 12c (paul geor), 14–15 (junxiao), 14 (thepalmer), 16–17 (monkeybusinessimages), 16 (piksel), 18 (jallfree), 20–21 (joelblit), 20 (markross).